Bible Verses for Children

ILLUSTRATED BY Robert S. Jones
EDITED BY Daphna Flegal
COPYEDITED BY Betsi H. Smith

Nashville

Sign and Say Bible Verses for Children

Copyright © 1998 Abingdon Press

ISBN 0-687-07442-8

00 01 02 03 04 05 06 07 – 10 9 8 7 6 5 4

MANUFACTURED IN THE UNITED STATES OF AMERICA

Sign, Say, and Remember

Children remember more easily what they learn when you involve both their bodies and their minds—and we want them to remember Bible verses! *Sign and Say Bible Verses for Children* will help your children learn Bible verses using the hand motions of American Sign Language. Use the simple steps listed below to learn these verses yourself and then teach the verses to your children.

- Look at the illustrations.
- Read the written directions.
- Practice, practice, practice! (You need to be able to sign the verse for the children without looking at the page.)

Thank you to Bob Geldreich and Peggy Jennings for their help with signing.

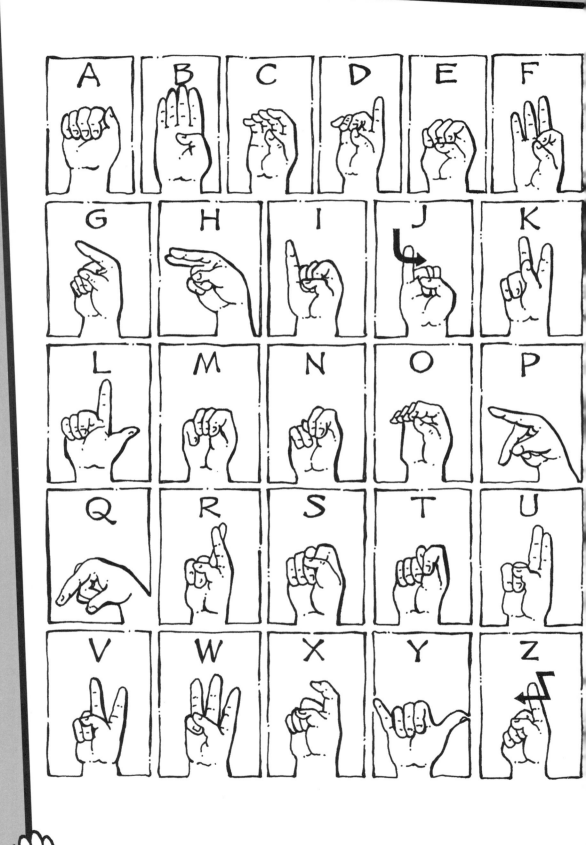

Contents

Old Testament

New Testament

Good news words

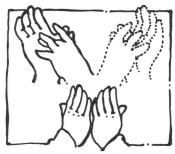

God said, "I will be with you."

Exodus 3:12, adapted

BIBLE VERSE:

God — Point the index finger of your right hand, with the other fingers curled down. Bring the hand down and open the palm.

I — Hold up little finger, with the other fingers curled down. Place at chest.

With — Hold both hands in fists, with thumbs on the outside. Place the fists together, palms touching.

You — Point out with your index finger.

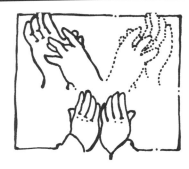

BIBLE VERSE:

You shall love the LORD your God with all your heart, and with all your soul, and with all your might.

Deuteronomy 6:5

You — Point out with your index finger.

Shall — Place your hand at cheek level, with the palm facing your cheek. Move hand forward.

Love — Cross hands at wrist and press over heart.

Lᴏʀᴅ — Make an "L" with the right hand. Place the "L" at the left shoulder and then move across the body to the right waist.

Gᴏᴅ — Point the index finger of your right hand, with the other fingers curled down. Bring the hand down and open the palm.

Aʟʟ — Hold the left palm toward the body. Circle right hand out and around the left palm. End with the back of the right hand in the open left hand.

Hᴇᴀʀᴛ — Draw an outline of a heart on the chest using index fingers.

Sᴏᴜʟ — Make an "O" with the left hand and place the hand close to the body. Touch the index finger to your thumb on the right hand. Place the right hand into the "O" of the left hand and then move right hand up.

Mɪɢʜᴛ — Place both fists over the right side of your chest. Move fists out.

9

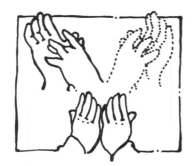

The LORD looks on the heart.

1 Samuel 16:7

BIBLE VERSE:

LORD — Make an "L" with the right hand. Place the "L" at the left shoulder and then move across the body to the right waist.

Lord

Look — Make a "V" with one hand. Place the "V" in front of the face, with the palm facing the face. Turn the "V" out so that the palm faces away from the face.

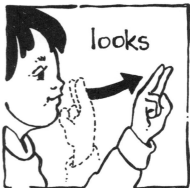

looks

Heart — Draw an outline of a heart on the chest using index fingers.

heart

© 1998 Abingdon Press

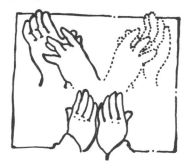

The LORD is my shepherd.

Psalm 23:1

BIBLE VERSE:

LORD — Make an "L" with the right hand. Place the "L" at the left shoulder and then move across the body to the right waist.

My — Open palm and place it on your chest.

Shepherd — Hold the left arm out. Place the right hand palm up on the left arm and make a cutting motion with the right fingers.

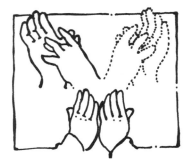

BIBLE VERSE:

The LORD is my light and my salvation.

Psalm 27:1

Lord — Make an "L" with the right hand. Place the "L" at the left shoulder and then move across the body to the right waist.

My — Open palm and place it on your chest.

Light — Bring both hands in front of body, with the fingertips touching the thumbs. Move the hands up and apart in front of each shoulder. Open hands and spread fingers apart as you move.

Salvation — Make fists with both hands, thumbs out. Cross hands at wrists. Turn fists forward and apart.

Lord

My

Light

Salvation

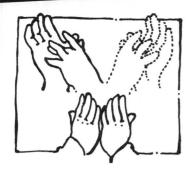

BIBLE VERSE:

Trust in the LORD.
Psalm 37:3

Trust

Lord

Trust — Make fists with both hands, thumbs out. Bring both fists to the left of your head. Have your right fist slightly below the left fist.

LORD — Make an "L" with the right hand. Place the "L" at the left shoulder and then move across the body to the right waist.

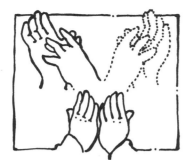

BIBLE VERSE:

Make a joyful noise to the LORD.

Psalm 100:1

Make — Make fists with both hands, thumbs out. Place the right fist on top of the left fist. Turn your fists so that the palms are facing your body. Touch the fists together again.

Joyful — Open both hands, with palms facing toward the chest. Pat the chest several times while moving the hands upward.

Noise — Touch the bottom of the ear with your index finger. Open both hands palms down, with fingers spread apart. Have the right palm behind the left palm. Move the hands toward the left.

LORD — Make an "L" with the right hand. Place the "L" at the left shoulder and then move across the body to the right waist.

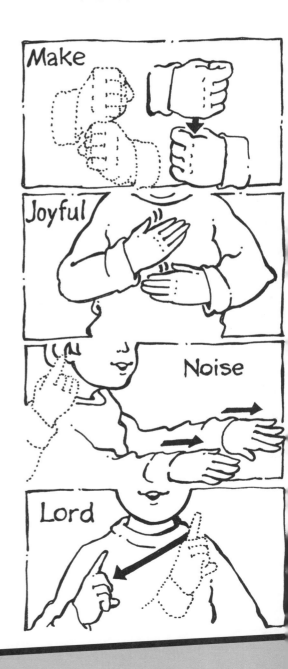

Make

Joyful

Noise

Lord

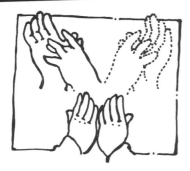

BIBLE VERSE:

Sing praise
to the LORD.

Psalm 105:2, adapted

© 1998 Abingdon Press

Sing — Hold the left hand out. Point the fingers of the right hand toward the left palm. Wave the fingertips back and forth over the left palm.

Praise — Clap your hands several times.

LORD — Make an "L" with the right hand. Place the "L" at the left shoulder and then move across the body to the right waist.

15

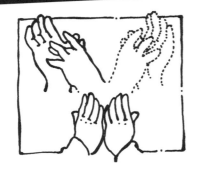

BIBLE VERSE:

I was glad when they said to me, "Let us go to the house of the LORD!"

Psalm 122:1

I

Glad

I — Hold up little finger, with the other fingers curled down. Place at chest.

Glad — Open both hands, with palms facing toward the chest. Pat the chest several times while moving the hands upward.

They — Point index finger forward and then move it to the right.

Said — Point right index finger. Hold finger in front of mouth and roll it forward.

Me — Point index finger of the right hand toward your chest.

Go — Point the index fingers of both hands, with one hand slightly behind the other. Move hands forward.

House — Touch the fingertips of both hands together. Bring hands apart and down to outline the roof of a house.

Lord — Make an "L" with the right hand. Place the "L" at the left shoulder and then move across the body to the right waist.

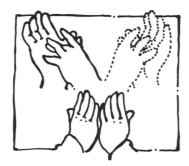

A friend loves at all times.

Proverbs 17:17

BIBLE VERSE:

Friend — Hook the right index finger over the left index finger. Reverse.

Loves — Cross hands at wrist and press over your heart.

All — Hold the left palm toward the body. Circle the right hand out and around the left palm. End with the back of the right hand in the open left hand.

Times — Tap the back of the left hand with the right index finger.

friend

loves

all

times

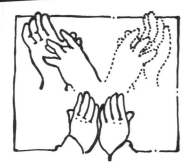

BIBLE VERSE:

For a child has been born for us.

Isaiah 9:6

 Child

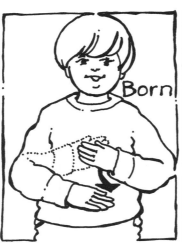 Born

 Us

Child — Place arms like holding a baby. Rock.

Born — Put the back of the right hand in the palm of the left hand. Move both hands forward and up.

Us — Touch your right shoulder with your index finger. Circle the finger out and then touch the finger to your left shoulder.

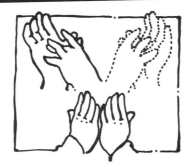

BIBLE VERSE:

Blessed are the peacemakers, for they will be called children of God.

Matthew 5:9

Blessed — Make a fist with both hands, thumbs out. Place both fists at the mouth. Bring hands forward and down, opening hands with palms down.

Peacemakers — Place the right palm on top of the left palm. Turn hands so that the left palm is on top of the right palm. Move both palms down and to the sides.

Hold hands open, with the palms facing each other in front of your body. Move both hands down.

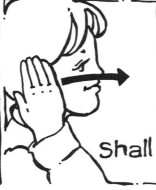

They — Point index finger forward and then move it to the right.

Will — Place your hand at cheek level, with the palm facing your cheek. Move hand forward.

Called — Extend first two fingers of both hands. Place the fingers of the right hand across the fingers of the left hand, forming an X. Move hands slightly up and forward, then down.

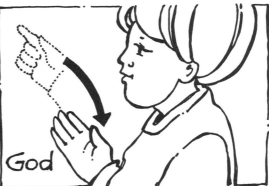

Children — Hold one hand palm down. Pretend to pat the head of child. Repeat several times.

God — Point the index finger of your right hand, with the other fingers curled down. Bring the hand down and open the palm.

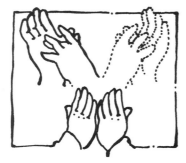

BIBLE VERSE:

You are the light of the world.

Matthew 5:14

the light of the world.

You — Point out with your index finger.

Light — Bring both hands in front of body, with the fingertips touching the thumbs. Move the hands up and apart in front of each shoulder. Open hands and spread fingers apart as you move.

World — Hold out three fingers on each hand (like a W). Circl the right hand around the left hand and plac the side of the right hand on the thumb of the left hand.

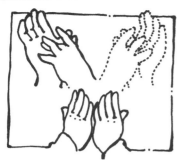
Give us this day our daily bread.

Matthew 6:11

Give — Touch thumb and fin-gertips on each hand. Have hands facing palm down. Turn hands palms up and flatten hands.

Us — Touch your right shoulder with your index finger. Circle the finger out and then touch the finger to your left shoulder.

Day — Extend the index fin-ger of the right hand. Place the right elbow at the left index finger. Move the right index finger in an arc until it touches the inside of the left elbow.

Daily — Make a fist with the thumb out. Rub the fist from the cheek to the chin several times.

Bread — Hold the left hand in front of the body. Move the lit-tle finger side of the right hand across the left hand as if slicing bread.

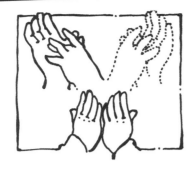

BIBLE VERSE:

Ask, and it will be given you; search, and you will find; knock, and the door will be opened for you.

Matthew 7:7

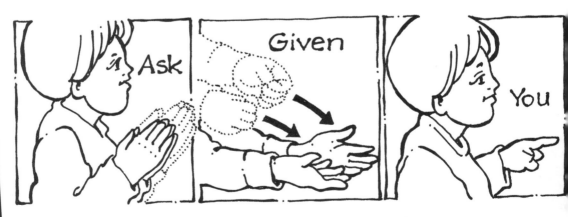

Ask — Hold hands palm to palm. Move palms toward body.

Given — Touch thumb and fingertips on each hand. Have hands facing palm down. Turn hands palms up. Flatten hands as you move them forward.

You — Point out with your index finger.

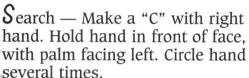

Search — Make a "C" with right hand. Hold hand in front of face, with palm facing left. Circle hand several times.

Find — Hold hand open, with palm down. Touch index finger to thumb and move hand up.

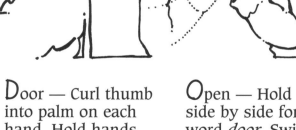

Knock — Hold left hand with the palm facing down. Rap back of hand with fist of right hand.

Door — Curl thumb into palm on each hand. Hold hands side by side, with palms facing forward.

Open — Hold hands side by side for the word *door*. Swing the right hand (thumb side) back and forth.

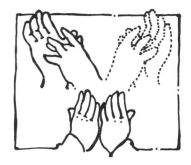

BIBLE VERSE:

Jesus said, "Follow me."
Matthew 9:9, adapted

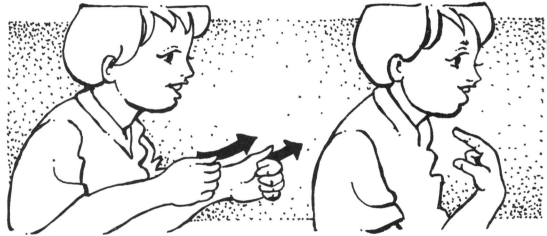

© 1998 Abingdon Press

Follow — Make a fist with both hands, thumbs out. Hold the right fist behind the left fist. Move both fists forward.

Me — Point index finger of the right hand toward your chest.

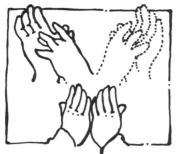

BIBLE VERSE:

Let the little children come to me.

Mark 10:14

Let — Hold hands with palms facing each other. Move the fingers up and out until the heels of the hands are closer together than the fingers.

Come — Extend index fingers on both hands. Circle fingers around each other toward the body.

Children — Hold one hand palm down. Pretend to pat the head of a child. Repeat several times.

Me — Point index finger of the right hand toward your chest.

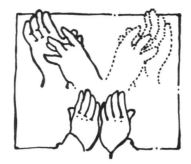

BIBLE VERSE:

Hosanna!

Mark 11:9

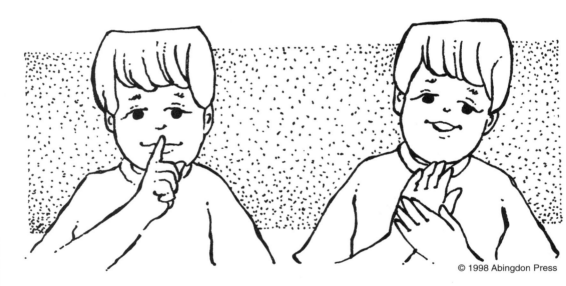

Hosanna — Touch the index finger of the right hand to the lips. Hold your left palm facing up. Make your right hand flat with palm facing down. Pat the right palm to the left palm.

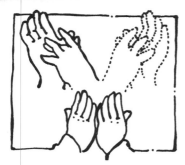

BIBLE VERSE:

You will name him Jesus.

Luke 1:31

*Y*ou — Point out with your index finger.

*N*ame — Extend first two fingers of both hands. Place the fingers of the right hand across the fingers of the left hand, forming an X.

*J*esus — Touch the middle finger of the right hand to the palm of the left hand. Reverse.

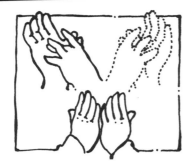

BIBLE VERSE:

I am bringing you good news of great joy for all the people.

Luke 2:10

I

bringing

you

© 1998 Abingdon Press

I — Hold up little finger with the other fingers curled down. Place at chest.

Bringing — Hold both hands palms up, with one hand behind the other. Move hands away from body.

You — Point out with your index finger.

Good — Touch fingers of the right hand to the lips. Move hand down and place it palm up in the left hand.

News — Touch tips of fingers and thumbs on each hand and place at forehead. Move hands down and away, End with palms up.

Great — Raise both hands up, with palms facing forward.

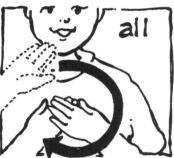

Joy — Open both hands, with palms facing toward the chest. Pat the chest several times while moving the hands upward.

All — Hold the left palm toward the body. Circle the right hand out and around the left hand. End with the back of the right hand in the open left hand.

People — Touch middle finger to thumb on each hand. Circle hands towards the center with alternating motions.

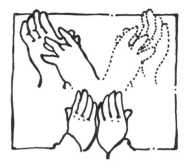

BIBLE VERSE:

Jesus grew both in body and in wisdom.

Luke 2:52, *Good News Bible*

Jesus — Touch the middle finger of the right hand to the palm of the left hand. Reverse.

Grew — Let the thumb and fingers of the left hand form an open circle, with the palm facing right. Push the right open hand up through the left hand.

Body — Touch your chest with both open palms. Repeat motion slightly lower on body.

Wisdom — Bend the index finger of the right hand. Move the bent finger up and down in front of the forehead.

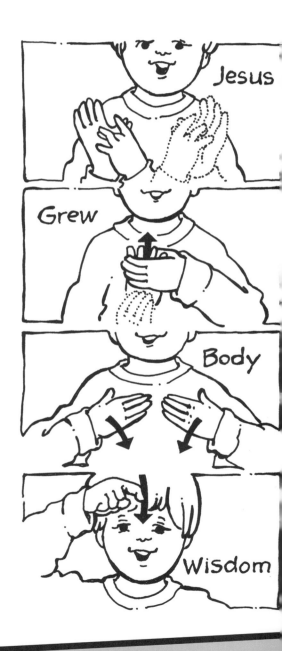

Jesus

Grew

Body

Wisdom

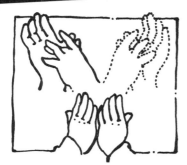

BIBLE VERSE:

Love your neighbor as yourself.

Luke 10:27, adapted

Love — Cross hands at wrist and press over heart.

Your — Hold up your hand, with the palm facing out.

Neighbor — Hold up both hands, with fingers slightly bent and palms facing the body. Move the right hand toward the inside of the left hand. Move hands to be parallel, with palms facing each other. Bring hands down.

Yourself — Hold hand in a fist, with the thumb out. Move fist quickly away from your body several times.

Love

Your

Neighbor

Yourself

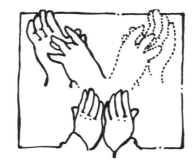

BIBLE VERSE:

For God so loved
the world that he gave
his only Son, so that
everyone who believes
in him may not perish
but may have eternal life.

John 3:16

God — Point the index finger of your right hand, with the other fingers curled down. Bring the hand down and open the palm.

Loved — Cross hands at wrist and press over heart.

World — Hold out three fingers on each hand (like a W). Circle the right hand around the left hand. Place the side of the right hand on the thumb of the left hand.

Gave — Touch thumb and fingertips together on each hand. Have hands facing palm down. Turn hands palms up and flatten hands as you move hands forward.

Only — Extend the index finger of the right hand. Hold the hand with the palm facing out and then twist the hand so that the palm faces the body.

Son — Bend fingers and thumb of the right hand as if grasping the bill of a hat. Place the hand at your forehead. Then bring the hand down to rest, palm up, inside the elbow of the bent left arm.

Everyone — Make fists with both hands, thumbs out. Hold up the left fist. Use the thumb of the right fist to stroke down the left thumb. Then hold up the index finger on right hand.

Believes — Touch your forehead with your right index finger. Bring hand down and flatten palm. Bring left palm up and clasp hands together.

Not — Make a fist with right hand, thumb out. Place thumb under chin and bring it forward.

Perish — Hold hands with right palm up and left palm down. Turn both hands over so that right palm is down and left palm is up.

Eternal — Point right index finger, palm up. Circle index finger in front of body. Change hand to hold out thumb and little finger, with palm facing down. Move hand forward.

Life — Extend the index finger and hold up the thumb to form an "L" with both hands. Move the "L" hands up in front of your body.

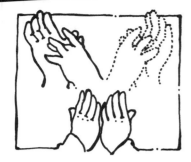

BIBLE VERSE:

Love one another.
John 15:17

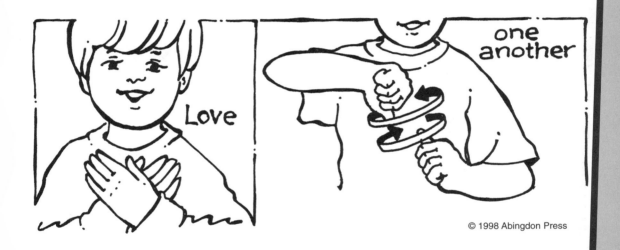

© 1998 Abingdon Press

Love — Cross hands at wrist and press over heart.

One another — Make a fist with both hands, thumbs out. Hold right fist with the thumb down. Hold the left fist with the thumb up. Circle the thumbs counterclockwise around each other.

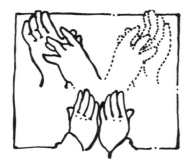

BIBLE VERSE:

Love is kind.
1 Corinthians 13:4

Love — Cross hands at wrist and press over heart.

Kind — Place the right palm over the heart. Move the hand up and around the left palm.

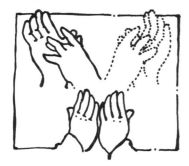

BIBLE VERSE:

Love never ends.

1 Corinthians 13:8

Love — Cross hands at wrist and press over heart.

Never — Hold right hand with palm out near right side of your chest. Circle hand across in front of left shoulder and move hand abruptly off to the right side of the body.

Ends — Extend the little fingers of both hands. Move the right little finger down to strike the end of the left little finger.

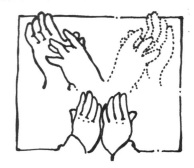

BIBLE VERSE:

Now faith, hope, and love abide, these three; and the greatest of these is love.

1 Corinthians 13:13

Faith

Hope

Faith — Hold out right index finger. Touch your forehead with your right index finger. Then make fists with both hands, thumbs out. Hold up the fists to the left of the face, with the left fist above the right fist.

Hope — Touch your forehead with your right index finger. Move right hand out in front of forehead and open hand with palm down. Bend fingers. Move left hand with palm down to in front of forehead on the left and bend fingers.

Love — Cross hands at wrist and press over heart.

Abide (Stay) — Hold the right hand with the little finger and thumb extended. Move hand down in a short movement.

Three — Hold up the thumb and first two fingers of your hand.

Greatest — Raise both hands up, with palms facing forward.

Love — Cross hands at wrist and press over heart.

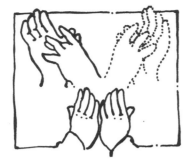

BIBLE VERSE:

Be kind to one another.

Ephesians 4:32

one
another

kind

© 1998 Abingdon Press

Kind — Place the right palm over the heart. Then move the hand up and around the left palm.

One another — Make a fist with both hands, thumbs out. Hold right fist with the thumb down. Hold the left fist with the thumb up. Circle the thumbs counterclockwise around each other.

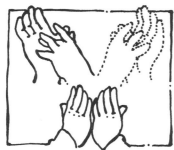

God cares for you.

1 Peter 5:7, adapted

BIBLE VERSE:

God — Point the index finger of your right hand, with the other fingers curled down. Bring the hand down and open the palm.

Cares — Move open right hand past your face and toward left shoulder. Repeat motion with left hand.

You — Point out with your index finger.

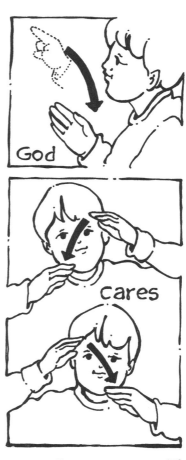

God

cares

you

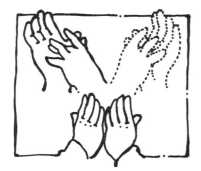

BIBLE VERSE:

God is love.
1 John 4:8

© 1998 Abingdon Press

God — Point the index finger of your right hand, with the other fingers curled down. Bring the hand down and open the palm.

Love — Cross hands at wrist and press over heart.

Thank you, God

Thank you — Touch fingertips to lips and then move hands down and back, one at a time.

God — Point the index finger of your right hand, with the other fingers curled down. Bring the hand down and open the palm.

Jesus loves me

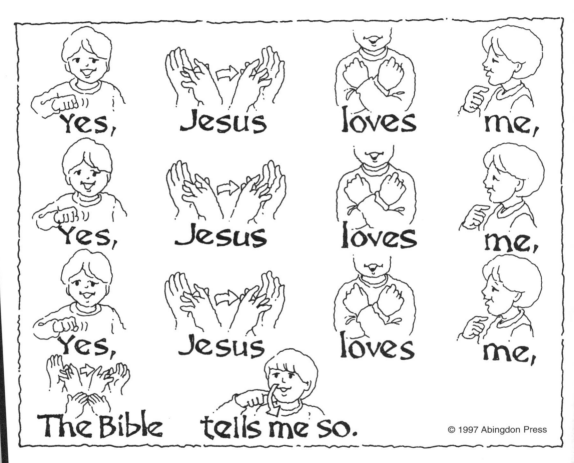

Yes, Jesus loves me,

Yes, Jesus loves me,

Yes, Jesus loves me,

The Bible tells me so.

© 1997 Abingdon Press

Jesus — Touch the middle finger of the right hand to the palm of the left hand. Reverse.

Loves — Cross hands at wrist and press over heart.

Me — Point index finger of the right hand toward your chest.

Alphabetical Index

Scripture Index

Old Testament

Exodus
God said, "I will be with you." (Exodus 3:12, adapted) — page 7

Deuteronomy
You shall love the LORD your God with all your heart, and with all your soul, and with all your might.
(Deuteronomy 6:5) — page 8

1 Samuel
The LORD looks on the heart.
(1 Samuel 16:7) — page 10

Psalms
The LORD is my shepherd.
(Psalm 23:1) — page 11
The LORD is my light and my salvation.
(Psalm 27:1) — page 12
Trust in the LORD. (Psalm 37:3) — page 13
Make a joyful noise to the LORD.
(Psalm 100:1) — page 14
Sing praise to the LORD.
(Psalm 105:2, adapted) — page 15
I was glad when they said to me, "Let us go to the house of the LORD!"
(Psalm 122:1) — page 16

Proverbs
A friend loves at all times.
(Proverbs 17:17) — page 18

Isaiah
For a child has been born for us.
(Isaiah 9:6) — page 19

New Testament

Matthew
Blessed are the peacemakers, for they will be called children of God.
(Matthew 5:9) — page 20
You are the light of the world.
(Matthew 5:14) — page 22
Give us this day our daily bread.
(Matthew 6:11) — page 23

Ask, and it will be given you; search, and you will find; knock, and the door will be opened for you.
(Matthew 7:7) — page 24
Jesus said, "Follow me." (Matthew 9:9, adapted) — page 26

Mark
Let the little children come to me.
(Mark 10:14) — page 27
Hosanna! (Mark 11:9) — page 28

Luke
You will name him Jesus.
(Luke 1:31) — page 29
I am bringing you good news of great joy for all the people. (Luke 2:10) — page 30
Jesus grew both in body and in wisdom.
(Luke 2:52, *Good News Bible*) — page 32
Love your neighbor as yourself.
(Luke 10:27, adapted) — page 33

John
For God so loved the world that he gave his only Son, so that everyone who believes in him may not perish but may have eternal life. (John 3:16) — page 34
Love one another. (John 15:17) — page 37

1 Corinthians
Love is kind. (1 Corinthians 13:4) — page 38
Love never ends.
(1 Corinthians 13:8) — page 39
Now faith, hope, and love abide, these three; and the greatest of these is love.
(1 Corinthians 13:13) — page 40

Ephesians
Be kind to one another.
(Ephesians 4:32) — page 42

1 Peter
God cares for you.
(1 Peter 5:7, adapted) — page 43

1 John
God is love. (1 John 4:8) — page 44

Good News Words
Thank you, God. — page 45
Jesus loves me. — page 46

48